Sermons For Pentecost III Based On First Lesson Texts For Cycle C

Buying Swamp Land For God

Robert P. Hines, Jr.

CSS Publishing Company, Inc., Lima, Ohio

SERMONS FOR PENTECOST III BASED ON FIRST LESSON TEXTS
FOR CYCLE C: BUYING SWAMP LAND FOR GOD

Copyright © 1997 by
CSS Publishing Company, Inc.
Lima, Ohio

Scripture quotations are from the *New Revised Standard Version of the Bible*, copyright 1989 by the Division of Christian Education of the National Council of the Churches of Christ in the USA. Used by permission.

Library of Congress Cataloging-in-Publication Data

Hines, Robert P., 1954-
    Sermons for Pentecost III based on first lesson texts for cycle C : buying swamp land for God / Robert P. Hines.
        p.   cm.
    Includes bibliographical references.
    ISBN 0-7880-1034-4 (pbk.)
    1. Pentecost season—Sermons.   2. Bible. O.T.—Sermons.   3. Sermons, American.
I. Title.
BV4300.5.H55   1997
252'.64—dc21   96-46507
                                                                                                          CIP

This book is available in the following formats, listed by ISBN:
    0-7880-1034-4   Book
    0-7880-1035-2   Mac
    0-7880-1036-0   IBM 3 1/2
    0-7880-1089-1   Sermon Prep

PRINTED IN U.S.A.

To Pat, Chris, and Erin,
my partners in ministry and life.

Editor's Note Regarding The Lectionary

During the past two decades there has been an attempt to move in the direction of a uniform lectionary among various Protestant denominations.

Preaching on the same scripture lessons every Sunday is a step in the right direction of uniting Christians of many faiths. If we are reading the same scriptures together, we may also begin to accomplish other achievements. Our efforts will be strengthened through our unity.

Beginning with Advent 1995 The Evangelical Lutheran Church in America dropped its own lectionary schedule and adopted the Revised Common Lectionary.

Reflecting this change, resources published by CSS Publishing Company put their major emphasis on the Revised Common Lectionary texts for the church year.

Table Of Contents

Buying Swamp Land
For God

Proper 21   *Jeremiah 32:1-3a, 6-15*
Pentecost 19
Ordinary Time 26

Years ago Art Linkletter had a portion of his show dedicated to showing us that kids will sometimes say the most unusual things. In a similar way, Allen Funt's *Candid Camera* showed us that people of all ages will sometimes do the strangest things. Well, the people of God have also been caught doing the strangest, most unusual things.

Abraham left his homeland and familiar surroundings to go to a land that God promised to give to him, a land he had never seen. Moses gave up his quiet life in the country to go back to Egypt, where he was wanted for murder, in order to lead the people of God out of their bondage.

David gave up his simple life as a shepherd to become king over Israel, even though it meant he spent much of his life on the battlefield.

Amos gave up his idyllic life as a farmer in order to speak the Word of God, a word of judgment, against the northern kingdom of Israel.

Peter, Andrew, James, and John gave up their lives as fishermen in order to follow Jesus, a decision that changed their lives in the most dramatic manner.

I'm sure there were some who thought these people were crazy for doing these things. They would have asked questions like these: "Why does Abraham want to leave town and go to some unknown place?" "Why would Moses put his liberty and life in jeopardy by going back to Egypt?" "Why would James and John leave their father in the boat and follow this stranger?"

When you do crazy things, you can expect people to wonder about your sanity, or at the very least, your sense of direction in life.

But of all the crazy things done by people in the Bible, perhaps the craziest was the action of Jeremiah as described in this passage. At the time this event took place, Jeremiah was in prison, put there because of his "treasonous" oracles. He had been telling the nation for quite some time that God was going to punish them for their sins. The leaders of the nation got tired of hearing this negativity, so they had him arrested.

About the same time, Babylon had invaded and surrounded the city of Jerusalem. The destruction that Jeremiah had predicted was taking place right before their eyes. It was a situation of deepest gloom and doom. The people were rightly terrified, and everyone was wondering what the future would hold for them. They knew that the Babylonian army was not known for its kindness and mercy. They didn't know if anyone would be alive when these events played themselves out.

In the middle of this gloomy, depressing time, Jeremiah decided to buy some property. Or we should say, God called Jeremiah to buy some land. While in prison, Jeremiah was visited by a kinsman of his, who invited the prophet to buy some land that he was selling.

According to Old Testament law, if a man was forced to sell some "family" land because of debt or poverty, the next of kin had the right and duty to buy the land and keep it in the family.

We can well imagine that with a mighty army outside the city gates, there probably weren't too many people investing in real estate. It's a bad time to buy land, when you're not sure who is going to be in control of things next week. In the ancient world, conquering armies tended to ignore deeds of sale. If they conquered your country, they figured they owned the land.

It was a time when there was no hope in the city of Jerusalem. People weren't planning for their retirement. They weren't even planning for next week. No one knew if anyone would be alive then. To buy land, when you could not be sure if you would be alive next week, was the height of folly. It was the dumbest investment Jeremiah could have made. People were probably saving their gold in order to buy themselves better treatment by the conquering Babylonians. But Jeremiah spent his gold on a piece of land. It was like he was buying swamp land.

What Jeremiah was doing, however, was very important. He was buying land to show that there was hope for the future of God's people. Even though he had predicted destruction and punishment, even though the agent of that destruction was outside the city walls, there was still hope for God's people. The future, although it may have been dark, still belonged to God. Buying that land was Jeremiah's way of telling and showing the people to put their trust in God. Jeremiah knew that the future of God's people does not depend on national security, or social security, or financial security. Our future depends on God. And because the future belongs to God, there is always reason to hope.

It is my contention that the people of God are often called to do things that look foolish to non-believers. We may be called to become foster parents after our own children are raised. We may be called to tithe when we can always find other things to do with that money.

We may be called to stand up to tyranny, as was Dietrich Bonhoeffer in Nazi Germany or Archbishop Oscar Romero in Central America. Bonhoeffer, along with other pastors of the Confessing Church in Germany, refused to obey the instructions of the Nazi government. He criticized Hitler and opposed the government at every turn. When he realized that there was only one way to stop Hitler's evil, Bonhoeffer joined a conspiracy to assassinate Hitler. He was arrested and imprisoned, and he was hanged just a few days before the Allies liberated his prison. His action may have been foolish, but he felt called to oppose tyranny and evil.

Oscar Romero was made Archbishop in El Salvador because the powers in control thought he was a quiet man who toed the line. They thought they could control him. But a funny thing happened to Romero when he became Archbishop. He began to feel the call of God to oppose the evil in his society, represented by the few wealthy families that owned almost all the land. He spoke out. He preached about justice and love. He called for reform. They couldn't shut him up. So they killed him. Romero was assassinated as he was celebrating the Lord's Supper. His behavior may have been foolish, but he felt called to oppose tyranny and evil.

We may feel called to take a stand on some issue, like abortion. Recently hundreds of Christians around the nation who oppose abortion lined the streets to protest our national policy that permits millions of human beings to be killed before they are born. Some thought this demonstration was foolish. But those who lined the streets felt called to speak out and let their voices be heard.

We may feel called to invest some of our money in socially responsible companies, even though the return may not be as great as with other companies who have no respect for the environment or workers' rights.

We may feel called upon to befriend someone in school or in the neighborhood who is despised by others.

God's people are often called upon to do things that may seem foolish. In fact, we sometimes call ourselves "Fools for Christ." We do these things because our hope for the future is based on Jesus Christ.

Our hope is not based on the solvency of Social Security or the United States government. Our hope is not based on the performance of the stock market and our own portfolio. Our hope is not based on the survival of some industry that provides us with employment. Our hope is not based on the survival of the mainline churches. Our hope is not based on our good health, or the success of our children. Our hope is based on Jesus Christ alone.

The Lord's Supper reminds us that God has been with us in the past, God is with us in the present, and God will be with us in the future. No matter what life may throw at us, God will be part of our future. That's why Jeremiah could buy land with the Babylonian army outside the walls of Jerusalem. And that's why we can follow the call of God that may seem outrageous and foolish to other people.

Whatever life may throw at us, we can handle it. Whatever we feel called to do, we can do it, because God is at work in our lives now, and will be with us in the future.

Our hope is based on Jesus Christ. That and that alone gives us the confidence to face each new day, and to follow the call of God into unknown and scary places.

Accepting Responsibility

Proper 22   *Lamentations 1:1-6*
Pentecost 20
Ordinary Time 27

There is a broad tendency in our culture to blame other people for our mistakes, to shift responsibility to someone else, to refuse to be accountable for the sins we commit.

One motorist filled out an insurance claim by stating that he was driving along, minding his own business, when a parked car got in his way.

Criminals will blame their behavior on their genetics and home life. This kind of blaming was carried to its most extreme form in the case of the Menendez brothers, who suggested in court that their father's abuse drove them to murder both their father and mother.

Children also play the blame game. One little girl was seen hitting her younger brother. When confronted with her behavior, the girl justified her action by claiming, "He made me do it. He wouldn't give me my doll."

The truth is that all of us often try to avoid responsibility for our behavior. And when bad things happen to us, we automatically look to blame someone else, something outside ourselves. When we flunk a test in school, it must be because the teacher did not like us, or the test was unfair. It was not because we did not study

13

for the test. When we get stopped for speeding, it must be because the cops are trying to generate extra income for the community. Surely, it was not because we were speeding. When our spouse walks out on us and asks for divorce, it must be because he or she is selfish. It is never because we did not do our part to make the marriage work. When bad things happen to us, we often try to escape responsibility for those bad things.

How different was the prophetic tradition in the Old Testament. Time after time, the prophets in the Bible warned the people of Israel that bad things would happen if they broke the covenant with God. And when those bad things happened, the prophets placed the blame squarely on the shoulders of the people. The fall of Jerusalem in 586 B.C. was the worst national disaster a person could imagine. The city of Jerusalem was captured by the Babylonian army, and the Temple of God was destroyed.

The people of Judah had come to believe that God would never let anything happen to their precious Temple. The Temple had been built with the blessing of God, and it was believed that it assured the people of God's presence and protection.

For many years, events in the world seemed to confirm their belief. After all, the northern kingdom fell in 722 B.C., but the southern kingdom survived the Assyrian threat. There were various threats from Egypt from time to time, but Jerusalem always managed to escape each danger.

Such was not to be the case in 586 B.C., however. The city was captured; the Temple was looted and destroyed; the best and the brightest of the people were taken into captivity. The worst disaster in the history of God's people had occurred.

It would have been easy to blame this disaster on something outside the nation. There may, indeed, have been some blaming of others, but not among the prophets. The prophets, including Jeremiah, placed the responsibility for the national disaster right where it belonged — on the shoulders of God's people. They were responsible for the fall of Jerusalem because they had sinned. The prophetic tradition would not let the people off the hook for this one. They had broken the covenant with God. The price they paid was the national defeat.

14

Jeremiah included these words in his lament: "Her foes have become the masters, her enemies prosper, because the Lord has made her suffer for the multitude of her transgressions" (Lamentations 1:5).

What we learn in this story is that there are consequences for our actions.

There is a popular parenting curriculum that emphasizes natural and logical consequences. Natural consequences are those things that occur naturally. If you throw a rock up in the air, the natural consequence is that it will come down. If you put your hand on a hot stove, the natural consequence is that you will get burned. If you do not brush your teeth, the natural consequence is that you will get cavities.

Logical consequences are those established by parents to teach their children lessons about responsibility. If you stay out past curfew, you may lose your car privileges as a result. If you do not pick up your toys, you may lose the right to play with them for a few hours. If you cannot control your temper, you may spend time in your room alone.

People need to learn that there are consequences for almost all our decisions and actions. If we have unprotected sex, there may be an unwanted pregnancy or a sexually transmitted disease. If we do not get to work on time, we may lose our job. If we spend more than we make, we may end up in bankruptcy court.

We also need to learn that there are consequences for our spiritual decisions and our behavior that relates to our faith. When we ignore our covenant with God, there are bound to be serious consequences. We may end up in our own kind of Babylonian captivity. We may find ourselves far from our source of strength and joy, wondering what went wrong.

I have talked to many people who used to be very active in the life of God's church. For some reason, they have slipped into inactivity. They talk with great fondness of the good times they had in the past when they were more involved. Most people cannot give a good reason for their present inactivity. But I can tell they are not happy about their situation. They would rather feel close to God again.

When we find ourselves in that situation, the tendency is to blame God for our problem. But, as the bumper sticker reads, when God seems far away, ask yourself, "Who moved?"

The story of God's people in the Old Testament shows that recovery for the Jews began when they took responsibility for their situation. When they were able to understand and admit that the Babylonian conquest was a result of their sin and failure to keep the covenant, they were on the road to recovery.

It is noteworthy that the Babylonian captivity was a highly significant period in the development of the Jewish faith. It was in Babylon that the synagogue arose as a way for Jews to practice their faith. When the temple was no longer available, the sacrificial system was replaced by a spiritual worship that emphasized the Word of God.

Good things came out of the Babylonian captivity, but only after the people acknowledged the role they had played in their national disaster. They had to accept responsibility for their sins before they could move on spiritually.

Lamentations is not a very happy book. It consists of five poems written during the exile. Each poem is an interpretation of the national tragedy of 586 B.C., designed to deepen the sense of personal responsibility. The writing and inclusion of this book in the Bible was one way for God's people to accept responsibility and continue the process of recovery from their tragedy.

There are bad things that happen to us all the time. Some of them can be blamed on other people or circumstances beyond our control. But many things that happen to us are our own responsibility.

We need to learn that there are consequences for our actions, especially in the area of our spiritual lives. If we ignore spiritual matters, we will pay a price. Often the price is tragic. We can become like the lonely widow pictured in Lamentations.

Recovery from any such tragedy begins when we accept responsibility for the part we have played in bringing the tragedy upon ourselves. Tragedy in our lives does not have to be fatal or irreversible. Often times, in the grace of God, those times can become opportunities for renewal, as the exile was for the Jews.

16

But that won't happen until we accept the blame that rightfully belongs to us.

Do you feel isolated from God? If so, let me ask you: Who do you think has moved? And what are you going to do about the distance that separates you?

Acknowledging your sin, your responsibility for the gap, is the first step on the road to recovering a close relationship with God.

Coping With Heartache

Proper 23   *Jeremiah 29:1, 4-7*
Pentecost 21
Ordinary Time 28

On the very first page of his book *The Road Less Traveled,* psychiatrist Scott Peck tells us something we know is true, but wish were not true, when he says, "Life is difficult."[1] Life is hard, and no matter how much we wish that life was easy, our wishing doesn't change it. Life is hard, and it is full of heartache.

Just this past week I received a mailing from a Christian organization that does mission work in Latin America. The director was sharing his troubles with the readers. The agency began the summer with a $40,000 deficit, and he was facing cancer surgery. By the end of the summer, he was getting his strength back, but they were $45,000 in the red.

Because he was facing seven weeks of radiation, the director decided to take a couple days off and get out of town. On the trip out of town, the motor of his car blew up. Five days later, he was home with a new motor in his car. He parked his car in front of his house, where it was promptly hit by an uninsured driver.

He decided to get the clothes washed, but the washer broke. His wife came down with bronchitis, and when he tried to install the new Windows 95 software into his computer, it wouldn't work.

The day he began his radiation treatments, he broke a cap off one of his teeth. And to top things off, he received a letter from Social Security saying he had made twice as much money as he actually did and therefore owed the government $6,000. This poor man had almost as much trouble as Job.

Even though our lives may not be as difficult as what this man experienced these last few months, anyone who has lived into adulthood will readily admit that life is full of heartache, trouble, and pain.

A husband and wife have to declare bankruptcy because of a business deal that went sour. Not only do they have to live with the embarrassment, but their credit rating is ruined for many years.

A girl comes home from school crying because she has once again been excluded by her friends. She was the only one who did not get invited to join a group that went to the local hangout for something to eat.

After pouring his life into his work for fifteen years, a man learns that the plant is closing and relocating to another state. He is not getting a chance to move with the plant. He loses his job.

After forty years of marriage, a man loses his wife to cancer. They had hoped to spend their retirement years traveling and visiting their children, but his wife's illness put an end to those dreams.

Everyone experiences emotional pain. There is no one who is immune. Sooner or later, we all have our own appointments with heartache. The question is how do we cope with this heartache?

The prophet Jeremiah lived during a time when the people of God in Judah experienced more than their fair share of heartache. Jeremiah lived and prophesied during the last years of the Davidic monarchy. During the early years of his ministry, Jeremiah preached a message of judgment and doom against his country. He spoke the Word of God when he accused the Jews of disobeying God's commands and rejecting the covenant.

During these early years of his ministry, political developments in the region made the situation more difficult for Judah. As Babylon began to flex its muscles, Judah stood in its way. There was no way Judah could stand up to the mighty Babylonian Empire, so in 597 B.C. the king of Judah surrendered. In what was the first wave of deportation, the king and much of the nobility were taken to Babylon, and the Temple and royal treasuries were plundered.

Nebuchadnezzar, the king of Babylon, installed Zedekiah as the new king of Judah. He was the last member of David's family to rule in Judah. Eventually, Zedekiah rebelled against Babylon and Nebuchadnezzar brought another army, captured Jerusalem, and this time destroyed both the city and the Temple in 586 B.C.

The letter to exiles from Jeremiah 29 was addressed to that first group of exiles that was deported in 597. Scholars estimate the letter was written in 594, suggesting that these exiles had lived in Babylon for about three years.

From the text we learn that there have been some prophets telling the people that this exile is going to be brief, and that the loss to Babylon was only a temporary setback. In essence, they were telling the exiles, "Don't accept this captivity as your reality."

Jeremiah had a very different interpretation of events. He understood that the Babylonian victory was the judgment of God. The people were being punished for breaking the covenant. And it was not something that was going to end soon. It was not an aberration, not a mistake, not a freak accident.

Jeremiah's advice to the first group of exiles was this: build houses, plant gardens, marry and have children, and seek the welfare of the community in which you live.

This was not what people wanted to hear. They wanted to hear that God would end their captivity, punish their enemies, and restore the nation to its greatness. They wanted to go back home!

But that's not what Jeremiah told them. He told them, "God is in control. There is a reason for these events. Accept them, and trust God to take care of you. God is still present and available to you in Babylon. Make the most of your life where you are."

Jeremiah's words are good advice to anyone who suffers heartache. So often, people spend a lot of time and energy wishing that unpleasant things had not occurred in their lives. We moan and groan about our problems and burdens, as if life should be easy. We long for the good old days, when we didn't have the problems that currently afflict us. We join in the universal litany of life: "If only...."

21

It doesn't matter how hard we wish for life to be different. Heartache is going to come into our lives! How do we cope with it? Not by wishing it away!

The first and most important step to recovery is acceptance. We can't go a step further until we accept the heartache and pain that happens in our lives. Once we accept what has happened, then we can begin to build the houses, plant the gardens, marry and have children, and get on with our lives.

What we have to understand is that no matter what happens, life goes on. It will go on with us or without us. It's our choice. We have to accept what happens in our lives.

I don't mean to suggest that acceptance is easy. Some things are very hard to accept. The death of a child, for example, is one of the most difficult things in life to accept. The fact that your mother or father didn't really love you is another. Some of these things are not easy to admit.

But there are two things which make it possible or easier to accept life and move on: the first thing is the knowledge that God is with us always.

The exile experienced by the Jews, though a great tragedy, may have been necessary in the development of the Jewish faith. So much had been invested in the Temple that the Jews could not imagine life without it. But spiritual life goes on, even without a temple. The only way for the Jews to learn that was through firsthand experience.

God was with the Jews in their Babylonian exile. They could still pray to God, and God responded. Though God may have brought that exile upon the Jews, God was still with them.

In a similar way, we may need to lose something or someone of great value to us in order to fully understand how God is with us always. Most people who are married would tell you that their spouse is a source of great blessing to them. But if our spouse dies, that does not mean God has deserted us. In the midst of our pain and emotional exile, God is still with us.

God doesn't always defeat or send the enemy away. But God is with us. God doesn't always cure our diseases, but God is still with us through our illnesses. God doesn't make our loved ones immune to death, but God is still with us.

22

Understanding how God is with us is the first thing that helps us accept what life throws at us. The second thing is the realization that whatever exile we may be experiencing will not last forever. There is always a brighter day in store for the people of God.

Although Jeremiah had to discount and refute the prophecies of those who said the exile wouldn't last long, he also assured the people that it would one day come to an end, at a time of God's choosing. In the meantime, the people had much to learn.

Now, if you know something is going to end, you can tolerate almost anything, even a bad sermon! Physical pain is easier to accept when we know it won't last forever. The emotional pain of a divorce is easier to tolerate when we know it's just temporary. Even the deep pain of losing a loved one is easier to accept when we understand that it gets better.

No matter how bad things may be, there is always hope for a better day, a brighter future, for the people of God.

There is nothing that will keep you from experiencing heartache. No one is immune to it. But these heartaches don't have to destroy us. Life goes on. We can build homes and plant gardens, marry and have children, because we know our God is with us, because we know our God helps us survive these heartaches, and because we know a better day will come. That knowledge helps us accept the bad things life sends our way. And acceptance is the first step to recovery. Acceptance of what happens is the only way to cope with heartache.

We can't go back and undo what has been done. We can't change the past. We have to accept where we are and start from this point. One minister I know puts it this way: "Bloom where you are planted." Make the most of the situation that life has placed you in. That was Jeremiah's message to the exiles in Babylon. And that is God's word to us.

---

1. M. Scott Peck, *The Road Less Traveled* (New York: Touchstone, 1980), p. 1.

The Heart
Of The Matter

Proper 24   **Jeremiah 31:27-34**
Pentecost 22
Ordinary Time 29

A number of years ago a man owned a red Ford Pinto station wagon. He bought it when he was going to college, and kept it for quite some time. In its last few years of service, the car had several thousand dollars put into it. The owner had to replace the engine; he had to put in a new transmission; and he had the whole body repainted. It looked good on the outside, but it had some serious problems on the inside.

The heart of the matter was that it was really on its last legs. When he finally bought a new car, the man traded in his Plymouth — a much nicer car. The dealer said he would give him $2,000 for it. Then the man asked the dealer to take a look at the Pinto. After taking it for a drive and inspecting it carefully, the dealer told the man he would give him $2,000 for both cars. The station wagon basically had to be scrapped.

That's the way it is with some things. Sometimes appliances or other items have so much wrong with them that they aren't worth fixing, or they can't be fixed. They simply have to be replaced.

That was the situation that faced the people of Israel back in the time of Jeremiah. Their relationship with God, based upon the events at the Red Sea and Mount Sinai, based on the Exodus event and the Law of Moses, wasn't working. They had tried for several hundred years to make the covenant work. But it just wasn't working out as God had intended.

Although God had been faithful to the covenant, the people of Israel had shown time and time again that they could not keep the requirements of the Mosaic covenant. They broke the law of God; they broke the heart of God.

Many of the prophets had been sent by God to warn the people to change their ways. If they didn't repent, they would be disciplined by God. Sometimes the warnings were heeded. But mostly they were ignored.

Jeremiah lived and ministered during the last years of the Kingdom of Judah. He was called to preach a message of judgment and doom because of the people's continual, willful disobedience. Perhaps no other prophet felt the pain, the anger, and the pathos of God as much as Jeremiah. He told the people that Jerusalem would be destroyed. Babylon would conquer the city of God. Nebuchadnezzar would violate the Temple that Solomon had built. This destruction would come because Israel could not, or would not, keep their part of the bargain.

Just how bad things were can be seen in the attitude of the exiles. The opening part of this passage, which was obviously addressed to those who had experienced the destruction Jeremiah had long predicted, quotes a proverb that was popular in those days: "The parents have eaten sour grapes, and the children's teeth are set on edge."

What the proverb means is that children suffer for the sins of their parents. Those who had experienced the destruction of their beloved Temple and city were blaming that event on the sins of their parents! Instead of owning up to their own responsibility and admitting that they had been wrong, that they had sinned, they were complaining that God was unjust, and that they were paying the price (unfairly) for the mistakes of their parents and grandparents.

But their behavior had brought their own destruction. They were responsible for what had happened, because if they had repented, they would not have witnessed the events of 586 B.C. Jeremiah always held some hope for a change of heart on the part of God. God would change his mind if the people repented.

Jeremiah, who had spent most of his career predicting the destruction of the city and Temple, now found himself called to offer comfort and hope to those who were hurting because of the Babylonian victory.

Jeremiah's message showed that the heart of the matter was that the old covenant didn't work and needed to be replaced by a new one. In verses 31 through 34, Jeremiah shares a message from God about a new covenant that God will make with the people.

This is one of the most important passages in the Bible. It represents the high point of Jeremiah's message, and one of the theological summits of the Old Testament. It was a passage that had great influence in the New Testament. It is quoted in Hebrews, and referred to in the Words of Institution for the Lord's Supper. In fact, it is because of this passage that the Bible's two parts are called the "Old" and "New" Testaments. It is a passage that the Church knows well.

In this promise of a new covenant, there are three promises made by God. And it is significant that the phrase "says the Lord" is used four times in the passage. This shows that the words are stamped with a high degree of divine authority. We can be sure of these three promises because the Lord has said they will occur.

In the new covenant, God promises to write the law of God on the hearts of the people. We know that the law of God was an important part of the old covenant made with Moses. The ten commandments were written on stone tablets, perhaps to suggest that they were unchangeable, and kept in the Ark of the Covenant. They were objects of veneration. The law was central to the Hebrew faith. And all the other laws that are included in the Old Testament gave shape and meaning to the decalogue. In essence, the other laws helped Israel understand what it meant to have no other gods, to honor your parents, to remember the Sabbath day, and so on.

The problem was not that the people of Israel did not understand what God wanted. The heart of the matter was that they really wanted something else. They wanted to decide for

27

themselves what was right and wrong, and so they disregarded the law of God at best, and they willfully disobeyed it at worst.

This was the heart of the conflict between the kings and the various prophets in Israel's history. Elijah opposed King Ahab because Ahab permitted and encouraged the worship of other gods in his kingdom. Elijah opposed the king because Ahab thought he could unjustly take the vineyard that belonged to Naboth. Idolatry and social injustice were two things banned by the law of God, but they were very prevalent in the kingdoms of Israel and Judah.

These sins of Ahab were not isolated events. The same sins were repeated again and again in the history of this people. What God wanted was not what the people wanted. And so they broke the law; they broke the covenant.

Through Jeremiah God promised that the new covenant will not be like that. God will put his law within his people so that they will want to do what God wants them to do. There will be no external code of behavior, no stone tablets, no need for a written law — because there will be a unity of wills. God's people will automatically do God's will because they will want to do so.

I know a family that just got a puppy at their house, and they've been working on house-training the dog. They have read a lot of books on the subject and talked to many people. One thing has been mentioned several times. Experts claim that the dog really wants to please its owner. It wants to do things that result in praise rather than a scolding. And, for the most part, this family has found that to be true. It's easier working with the dog when it wants to do what we ask of it. I can't imagine working with an animal that willfully does things to displease its owner.

It must have caused the Lord great distress to find that the people of Israel did not want to obey God's commands.

To understand how awful that can be, just recall the times you have seen a screaming child in a store begging for something on the shelf and a parent who is refusing to give it to the child. It can be an ugly scene. Or imagine trying to drive an automobile that has a will of its own, a car that doesn't respond to your direction. Wouldn't that be a nightmare? Or imagine employees who don't do what you ask of them, but do what they want, even if it's wrong.

God and Israel had had that kind of experience and it ended in heartache and pain. But in the new covenant, God will write the law on the hearts of the people. They will want to please God. They will want to do the will of God. There will be no contest of wills, no conflict of interest. Doing the will of God will be part of their nature. That is the promise of God.

In the new covenant, not only will the people of God want to do God's will, but it is promised that they will know God. Knowing God is an important prophetic theme. Ignorance of the Lord is a frequent criticism made by the prophets. It was Hosea who said, "My people are destroyed for lack of knowledge ..." (Hosea 4:6). People had forgotten that it was God who had redeemed them and continued to sustain them. They had forgotten the law of God and so were living in ignorance.

In the new covenant that will not be the case. Everyone will have knowledge of God, from the greatest to the least. It will not be necessary for some people to teach others about the Lord. There will be no need for Sunday school, Bible studies, seminaries, expository sermons, or Bible commentaries. In the new covenant, people will know God in an intimate, personal way.

The passage suggests this knowledge of God will be similar to the knowledge of God experienced by the prophets. It will be that personal, that intimate.

One of the problems we have in our society, and in our churches, is that so many people confuse knowledge about God with knowledge of God. Knowledge about God is what we learn from books, from parents and teachers, from video tapes, and from preachers. It is secondhand knowledge. A person can have a lot of this kind of knowledge about God and still not know God in a personal way, from firsthand experience.

You could answer every question on the Jeopardy board in the Bible category and still not have a living relationship with God. That's knowledge about God. And it has very little use in life.

But personal knowledge of God comes from a relationship with the Lord. We get this knowledge when we invite Jesus to become the Lord and Savior of our lives. Only when we make that commitment do we begin to know the Lord in a personal way.

A father took his young son to a major league baseball game along with one of the father's friends. The father's friend had a son who was a pitcher for one of the major league teams. It was the father's intention to stay after the game and have his friend's son introduced to his own boy.

After the game, the trio made their way to the locker room door and waited for the players to come out. As they waited for his friend's son to come out, some of the star players pushed away the fans and made a dash for their cars.

Other players came out and signed autographs, but the boy didn't really get to talk to any of them. But when his father's friend's son came out, because the lad was with his dad, the player took the time to shake his hand, to talk to him, and to greet him as a real human being.

After that experience, the young boy paid a lot of attention to that player's career. He did so because he felt he had a relationship with the player. He had met him face to face, and that made all the difference.

Our knowledge of God in this life is very limited. We need to have other people teach us about God. That's how we get introduced to the Lord. But some of us are content with this second-hand knowledge, and this creates problems. We are not as intimate with the Lord as we need to be.

But in the new covenant, Jeremiah claimed that all God's people will have firsthand, full knowledge of God. That's a promise.

The third promise for the new covenant is that forgiveness of sin will be abundant. It will be a time of boundless grace, limitless love, incomprehensible forbearance.

Please note: God does not promise that in the new covenant people will be perfect, or that they will be sinless. God promises to forgive and to forget their iniquity. That suggests there still will be mistakes and problems. But forgiveness will be the rule of thumb. Grace will be more important than sin.

It has been suggested that forgiveness gives us a new sense of worth, and with this sense of worth comes a desire to be worthy. A sense of worth, a sense of self-esteem, has tremendous regenerative power. When we feel good about ourselves, our actions tend to be positive, wholesome, and edifying to others. It is when we feel bad about ourselves that we engage in destructive, hurtful behavior.

Billy was the youngest of three children born to a woman who became addicted to heroin. The children did well to survive. There were many nights when their mother never came home. There were days when there was no food in the house. They often wore dirty clothes.

Billy didn't feel very good about himself. This negative self-image was reflected in his behavior toward others. He was a problem at school. He always seemed to get into trouble.

When he was eight years old, the state took the children away from their mother, and placed them in a foster home. For the first time in their lives, those children knew that someone cared for them. They had clean clothes, good food, and adults who set limits on their behavior.

In six months Billy changed from being a problem student to a model student. Feeling good about himself encouraged him to live a life that would make others proud.

The best news the people of Israel who were in exile could hear in those days was the fact that the new covenant was going to be based on forgiveness and grace. By being grounded in God's willingness to forgive, both the power and the permanence of the new covenant was assured.

In the new covenant there are three promises that we hold dear: God promised to write God's law on the hearts of God's people; God promised that all God's people will have intimate knowledge of God that comes from a personal relationship, and God promised to build that covenant on forgiveness and grace.

Comparing the new covenant to the old, we see that there are no more "if" clauses in the new. In the covenant made with Moses, there were all kinds of conditions attached to the promises. If the people obeyed God's law, they would prosper in the new land. The history of Israel showed that people just aren't capable of keeping that kind of covenant. We just can't do it.

God, in God's goodness and grace, therefore decided to make a new covenant. This one has no conditions, no "if" clauses. The heart of the matter is that it is built on grace, not law.

We understand that in Jesus Christ the new covenant has come into being. Forgiveness of sin is the basic message of the gospel. That's why we declare to the community every week this phrase: "Friends, believe the good news of the gospel: in Jesus Christ we are forgiven." Our knowledge of God may be imperfect, but we know all we really need to know. We're not perfect, but we do want to please the Lord with our lives.

The heart of the matter is this: we aren't sure why we should be, but we're forgiven, and in Christ we're moving toward what God wants us to be.

Permission
To Daydream

Proper 25   *Joel 2:23-32*
Pentecost 23
Ordinary Time 30

Manny pictured it in his mind. He would go to Harvard Law School and graduate with highest honors. He would come back home and run for office: mayor, state representative, governor, and finally, president of the United States. He could see himself doing important things in politics, helping people in significant ways. He would fight poverty, repair bridges and highways, clamp down on crime, and negotiate peace in different parts of the world. When he saw these things happen in his mind, a great big smile of contentment and pleasure emerged on his face.

Miss Stevenson, his fifth grade teacher, was not so amused that Manny was daydreaming again. The spell was broken when she called on him to answer the math question she had on the board. Before he became president, Manny would have to get through fifth grade.

Dreams are important in our lives. They are important because, in the words of Eugene Peterson, "they organize the present and direct its energies to future fulfillments."[1]

No one ever becomes president without first dreaming of being president. No one ever goes to medical school without first envisioning oneself going there. No one ever builds a house without first getting a picture of it in mind and then on paper. No one climbs the highest mountain without first dreaming of doing so.

Being created in the image of God suggests many things. One of the things it suggests is that we have the ability to imagine a better world. We have the power to dream of a better life. We have the capability of visualizing ourselves doing great things.

A person who has no dreams for life is in serious trouble. Without a dream, there is no direction, no motivation, no passion. And a people or nation without a dream is a nation headed for disaster.

The prophet Joel wrote three short chapters that got included in our Bible. We don't know much about this prophet. There is very little in his writing that gives us solid clues as to the exact time of his ministry, and he is not mentioned outside of his own writings.

The best scholarly guess is that Joel prophesied in Judah during the reign of King Uzziah (792-740 B.C.). These were days of great prosperity and national success. Uzziah expanded his territory and seized control of the caravan routes in the area. He improved fortifications in the kingdom and reorganized the army. It was a time that harkened back to the reign of Solomon in terms of its prosperity.

In the midst of this prosperity, the people of Judah experienced a locust plague without parallel. It was so devastating that all levels of society were affected.

Joel saw this plague as the judgment of God. The locusts were a warning that even greater judgment was coming unless the people repented.

The basic message of the prophet was that God's people need to repent. The people who heard this message were people who had experienced a devastating plague. Their prosperity was severely threatened, and they were scared. In fact, these people were so shaken by the events of this natural catastrophe that their ability to envision a brighter future was seriously impaired. They needed a word of encouragement.

34

So, in addition to his message of repentance, Joel also had a word of hope. That word of hope is contained in our scripture reading for today. To a people who were experiencing a disastrous plague, the prophet Joel had three things to say.

The first thing he made clear in his proclamation was that God is sovereign. God is in control — of nature and history. This is a central biblical concept, one that runs throughout scripture. There may be kings and queens, but God controls the destiny of nations. The pagans may offer sacrifice to Baal, but God is in charge of the rain, the sun, and the harvest. People may look to the starry constellations for clues as to their destiny, but God is in control. God is sovereign.

This is a message we need to hear when our world seems to be falling apart. When the car breaks down for the third time in a week, or when it snows another six inches on top of the six already on the ground, or when our football team loses a big game, we need to remember God is in control. We don't control God. Our prayers may influence God. Our gifts may please God. But God doesn't take orders from us.

The people of Israel had a special relationship with God, a relationship that they traced all the way back to Abraham. Because they viewed themselves as the "chosen" people of God, they tended to view everything through the lenses of chosen-ness. "Chosen" came to mean blessed, protected, and superior.

This attitude is evident in the popular idea of the "Day of the Lord." This was the day they expected Yahweh to come and make his Lordship known fully to all the earth. For the people of Israel it had come to mean a day when all their enemies would be judged and punished, and Israel would be exalted. It would be a day of vindication, a day of vengeance, a day of rejoicing over their enemies.

Joel and the other prophets, however, had a different vision for the Day of the Lord. They pictured it as a day of terrible judgment for Israel! The locusts were just a harbinger of terrible things to come.

Joel wanted the people to understand that they could not control God with their grand expectations for the Day of the Lord. They could not control God with their sacrifices and sacred rituals. God will not be put in a box and confined to our expectations. God is sovereign.

It is the particular hubris of the modern age to think that we can master our universe. We build magnificent roads and bridges; we construct fuel-efficient cars and homes; we fly faster than the speed of sound, and can walk on the moon. We've come a long way, and there is a tendency to think we have mastered our environment.

But all it takes is a hurricane or a tornado, a flood or a snowstorm to remind us that we aren't so masterful. There are things beyond our control. That's what the people of Judah discovered in the plague of locusts. That's what we need to remember when we experience both good and bad times. God is sovereign.

The second thing Joel had to say was that the people of God have a promising future. No matter how bad the plague was, God had good things in store for the people of Judah. God promised the rain would return, the locusts would leave, and the harvest would be abundant. The catastrophe would not last forever.

This is a word for us as well. No matter how bad a situation may be for us, we have a future filled with promise. There are no limits to the things we can do with God's help. As Paul said, "I can do all things through him who strengthens me" (Philippians 4:13). There is no mountain we cannot climb. There is no problem we cannot solve. There is no injury we cannot cure. When we depend on God's strength, we can do anything. We have a future filled with promise because God is a part of our future.

We have our own version of the locust plague. It may be the death of a loved one, the onset of a serious illness, the loss of a job, or the failure to make the cheerleading squad, to get the lead in the school musical, or to get into the college of our choice.

Any of these things can really knock us down. But none of these things is fatal. Oh, yes, they hurt. Make no mistake about that. But the damage they do isn't permanent.

The resurrection of Jesus Christ is the greatest confirmation of the promise that we have a bright future. Not even death can keep God from doing what is best for us.

Because God is sovereign, we have a future filled with promise. What Joel proclaimed is for this life and beyond. He promised that they would once again see rain and experience an abundant harvest. That's something that came true in just a short while. Natural catastrophes are devastating, but they don't usually last a long time.

But Joel went on to say something about a time when God's spirit will be poured out on all flesh. He promised a time when old and young alike will dream dreams and see visions. He foresaw a time when all people who call upon the name of the Lord will be saved.

This has been a significant text in understanding the story of Pentecost, the birthday of the Church. Peter seems to have understood that with the coming of the Holy Spirit at Pentecost, the prophecy of Joel was fulfilled. On that day people prophesied and spoke in foreign languages. People from all around the world heard the word of God proclaimed, and many believed in the name of Jesus that day.

Pentecost was a kind of provisional fulfillment of Joel's prophecy. That kind of power has not been repeated in the history of the church, and it certainly has not been our everyday experience. In essence, Pentecost showed us what is going to happen when Joel's prophecy is ultimately fulfilled in the Kingdom of God. It gave a foretaste of the wonder that is to come, and in the process, equipped the early Church for its mission.

We live on this side of Pentecost, after the Spirit has been given, which means we have the power to carry out our calling. But we also live in expectation of the final fulfillment of this marvelous vision that will come on the Day of the Lord.

Because God is sovereign, and because God has given us the Spirit to do God's calling, we have a future filled with promise. Nothing in life can defeat us, if we draw our strength from God.

Finally, because God is sovereign, and because we have a future filled with promise, we are free — free to dream, free to envision a brighter tomorrow, free to imagine the Kingdom of God in all its fullness!

One of the problems we have in our age is that so many people have forgotten how to dream, or have given it up, or have traded their altruistic dreams in for selfish ones.

A few decades ago America dreamed of bringing an end to poverty. We have given up on that dream, and now we dream of balancing the budget.

My generation once dreamed of changing the world, making it a better place. Many are now simply dreaming of saving enough money to retire in comfort.

The mainline churches once dreamed of leading all the people of the world to Christ by the year 2000. Now many are just dreaming of surviving, meeting the budget, getting enough people to serve as officers.

One of the problems we have is that we are not dreaming the dreams of God. Someone has told us to stop daydreaming, and we are listening to that voice.

It doesn't have to be that way. If we understand that God is sovereign, we don't have to fear the future. We are free to envision it. Because we know the future belongs to God, we are free to see ourselves as part of it. We must not give up our dreams. We are called to dream the dream of God.

It is important that we envision the future in this way because the act of dreaming itself is an act of courage in a fallen world. The act of dreaming shows faith in God and leads us to take the next step of doing what we can to make the dream come true.

Many years ago Martin Luther King, Jr., gave a speech in which he declared that he had a dream, a dream of an America where all God's children would live in peace and justice. That dream propelled the civil rights movement. That dream empowered us to change as a nation. That's the power of a dream.

There are forces in the world that do not want us to dream or have visions. These forces would like nothing better than for us to be content with the way things are, or to be so discouraged that we give up hoping for a better day.

Teachers sometimes correct their students for daydreaming. But God gives us permission to dream. God gives us the Spirit so that we may dream. God calls us to dream.

To dream, to envision a future filled with promise because God is sovereign, is an act of faith, and perhaps it is the most radical thing we can do in a fallen world.

---

1. Eugene Peterson, *Five Smooth Stones for Pastoral Work* (Grand Rapids: William B. Eerdmans Publishing Company, 1980), p. 69.

Possession Is Nine-tenths
Of The Law

All Saints' Day   *Daniel 7:1-3, 15-18*

The book of Daniel belongs to that strange genre of biblical literature we call "apocalyptic." To the modern ear it sounds very different, and its language is somewhat bizarre. Some interpreters have tried to use this literature to predict with certainty the future, but some find this to be an inappropriate use of scripture. Apocalyptic literature is much easier to understand, and more helpful to us in our daily living, if we avoid trying to use it as a detailed outline of future events and simply try to understand what it was intended to say to its original audience.

Biblical scholars disagree concerning the date and authorship of the book of Daniel. The setting in the story is the Babylonian exile, and some consider that period to be the time of authorship. Others think Daniel was written during the time of the oppressive regime of the Seleucid Empire, during the period of the Maccabean rebellion in Judea.

When Alexander the Great died in 323 B.C. at the age of 32, his kingdom was divided into three sections, each ruled by one of his generals. The area around Babylon and Syria was ruled by Seleucus, who founded a dynasty that ruled the area for about 200 years. The successors of Alexander the Great were intent on imposing Greek culture on all the conquered nations, and they did so to a large degree. It was this policy that led to serious problems in Judea.

The Seleucids gained control of Palestine around 223 B.C., and Antiochus IV pushed the policy of imposing Greek culture on the Jewish people with a vengeance. He insisted that the Jews worship Zeus, and after the Jews rebelled against this idea, Antiochus came to Judea to punish the rebels. An altar to Zeus was erected in the Temple, and on that altar were sacrificed swine, the most unclean animals according to the Jewish law. Other pagan altars were erected all over the land, and Jews were required to sacrifice to Zeus and eat pig's flesh.

This was the worst persecution the Jews had ever faced. They had endured military conquest and political domination, but until this time no conqueror had tried to impose a foreign religion on the Jewish people.

It may have been in the midst of this severe political domination and religious persecution that the book of Daniel was written. If so, then it was written at a time of extreme national distress, when the Jewish people wondered if God was in control. Psalm 74 expresses the depth of anguish felt at this time, when it asks the question: "O God, why do you cast us off forever? Why does your anger smoke against the sheep of your pasture?"

If Daniel was written earlier, during the time of the Babylonian exile, then the situation was similar. The nation had endured a terrible defeat that had called into question all the assumptions about their relationship with God. If God is sovereign, then why were the gods of Babylon, or the gods of Greece, allowed to gain control over God's people in Judea? It was a crisis of faith, either during the Babylonian exile, or during the Seleucid rule, that led to the writing of Daniel.

There is no question that the author of Daniel intended the four beasts of his vision to represent the cruel and harsh kingdoms of the ancient world that had oppressed the Hebrew people. These extensive empires were built on the bloodshed of countless innocent people. When cities were captured, it was not unusual for the conquering army to slaughter much of the population, or sell the people into slavery. War was not pretty, and to be conquered was not a pleasant fate.

The imagery used by Daniel suggests the savagery of these kingdoms. One is pictured as a lion with wings like an eagle. Another is pictured as a bear with ribs of another creature in its mouth. The third is pictured as a four-headed, winged leopard. The last one is worst of all — a beast unlike any other creature, with ten horns and teeth of iron.

The Jewish people had faced the worst the world could throw at them. They had seen their holy city and precious temple destroyed in 586 B.C., and then they had seen the new temple desecrated by the building of an altar to Zeus. They had seen their loved ones killed, and experienced an exile in a foreign land. This was a nation that knew from firsthand experience the deepest tragedy inflicted by powerful enemies. The Jewish people had been defeated and conquered, persecuted and oppressed, afflicted and tyrannized.

As a nation we have not had those kinds of experiences. We are so blessed as a people. We have not had a foreign army on our soil since the War of 1812. We've never really lost a war, nor have we had to surrender to an enemy. We've never had a foreign power come in and tell us that we can't worship the way we want to, or impose a system of religion on us. The beasts of Daniel's vision find no political or military equivalent in our lives.

But that is not to say we don't face our own kind of beasts. Anyone who has ever had a drinking problem will tell you what an oppressive power alcoholism can be. Anyone who has ever been unemployed for a lengthy time can tell you what a serious tyrant unemployment can be. Anyone who has ever been told he has cancer will tell you how devastating that illness can be.

We may not face the beasts that the Hebrews faced, but we have our own beasts and monsters in this life.

The thing that all the cruel kingdoms of the ancient world and all superpowers of the modern era have in common is the belief in their own power and ultimacy. Those ancient empires believed that they were in control of history. Modern superpowers have shared in that belief also.

Nazi Germany won a few early victories and came to believe that they were a nation destined to rule the world. In a similar way, Japan believed in the certainty of their victory in World War II because of their destiny as a nation.

If we think of our beasts as having awareness and sentient existence, they, too, share this belief in their ultimacy and power. It may be helpful to think of our beasts in this way, as the apostle Paul reminded us that we wage a war against principalities and powers, not just flesh and blood.

When we are in the grips of a terminal illness, or prolonged unemployment, or depression, or financial ruin, or addiction, these things have tremendous power over us. And if they are principalities and powers, then they do, indeed, think they have control of our lives. They think they are the last word in life. Anyone going through one of these experiences will tell you this.

But the good news of the gospel, and the message of Daniel, is that these things don't have that kind of power. They don't have the last word, after all. The last word belongs to God.

As Daniel's vision is explained to him, despite the fact that four great kingdoms do arise, in the end, the saints of God will receive the kingdom and possess it forever.

The vision of Daniel does not tell us the beasts or kingdoms of this world have no power. Their power is real, and their ability to hurt us is real, but this power is not ultimate.

Ultimacy belongs to God alone. The one really in control is God. The one who decides the destiny of people and nations is God. And in the end, it will not be the four beasts that possess the kingdom; it will be the saints of God — you and me, and those that have gone before us, and those that come after us who live by faith.

When I sit beside someone in a hospital room, and we consider the ravages of cancer and the swift approach of death, it is reassuring to remember this promise that cancer does not have the last word, that the saints will possess the kingdom. When I counsel with someone who is lost in a surfeit of emotional pain, it is helpful to remember this promise that this pain does not have the last word, that the saints will possess the kingdom. When I go through my own deep valleys of darkness, it is helpful to remember this promise that darkness is not the last word, that the saints will possess the kingdom.

In our culture we have a saying that "possession is nine-tenths of the law." That suggests that it doesn't matter what you say about some article or item. The person who actually possesses it has a better chance of keeping that article. If a dispute of ownership ends up in court, the one who has possession is the one most likely to keep it, unless another person has proof of ownership. It is possession that counts.

The principalities and powers of this world, the evil things that happen to us, think they own us. They think they can control our lives completely.

But we will possess the kingdom. The saints of God will be given the power. Not because we deserve it. Not because we have done something to earn it. But because God is sovereign. Because God is in control. Because God is the Lord of history. And because it is God's will that we be given the kingdom.

The beasts have their existence. They have their power over us for a time. They may even think they have the last word. But such is not the case. The last word belongs to God. The kingdom will be ours.

This gives us hope as we face our monsters and beasts. They may afflict us with pain, but they can't defeat us. They may bruise and wound us, but they can't kill our spirit. They may beat us down and cause distress, but they cannot win the war!

Possession is what counts. The kingdom belongs to us. And we belong to God. Thanks be to God!

The Burdens
Of The Past

Proper 27   *Haggai 1:15b—2:9*
Pentecost 25
Ordinary Time 32

Recently a young man who participates in Civil War reenactments was giving a talk about his hobby. He shared with the group how a soldier in that war carried his own food supply with him. A bag of food weighed about seven pounds. The rifle he carried weighed ten pounds. The blanket and backpack weighed another forty pounds. This means the typical soldier in the Civil War carried over fifty pounds of material and weaponry with him all the time. Carrying that much weight must have been a heavy burden that made marching from one area to another very tiresome.

The veterans of more recent wars can probably tell of similar loads they carried in their time of service. And students in today's schools can also tell us about burdens they carry. Most children today carry their books in backpacks. A recent story on the news showed how some students have experienced back, neck, or shoulder problems because of the heavy burdens they carry in those packs. It can be a special problem if the students carry the load on just one shoulder, but even if balanced equally, it can be quite a load.

Burdens that we carry can cause all kinds of problems. They slow us down, they cause pain and discomfort, and they make it difficult to do some things we'd like to do.

It will come as no surprise to you that there are spiritual and emotional burdens just as bad as any physical burden we may experience in life. And these spiritual and emotional cargoes can be far more harmful and have a more negative impact on our lives than any physical burden.

When the prophet Haggai ministered to the Jewish people, they were carrying a tremendous spiritual and emotional burden that was keeping them from experiencing the goodness of God. The time that Haggai ministered to the Jews was around 520 B.C., about seventy years after the Babylonian victory that had destroyed the Temple and sent the best and brightest of the nation into exile.

When Cyrus, the King of Persia, conquered Babylon, he decreed that the Jews could return home. Zerubbabel, the heir to the throne of David, and Joshua, the high priest, were the leaders of the people who had returned to Judea.

It had been some time since the Jews had returned, and Haggai had to remind them to get started on the Temple. That message is contained in his first oracle, in chapter one. In the second chapter, Haggai deals with the burdens of the past that were preventing this work from progressing.

Most of the people who had returned from Babylon had probably not seen Solomon's temple. That was destroyed seventy years prior to their return. But they must have heard stories about the Temple. They must have heard all about the opulence and grandeur of that temple. And then they looked at what they were building and must have gotten terribly discouraged. What they were building wasn't anything like Solomon's temple. They didn't have the resources that Solomon had.

And some must have wondered and asked the question: "What is the point? This one will never be as grand as the first temple." Their focus on what had been, the former glory, kept them from moving forward. They needed to let go of the past because it was keeping them from moving on with their lives.

Do we not see the same thing today? Clinging to the past keeps some people from moving on. Sometimes it is a wonderful, glorious past that is the culprit. When we prefer the good old days so much that we don't deal with today's reality, it becomes a serious problem.

A church in the heart of the city had a significant history. At one time it was the most prestigious church in the community. Many civic leaders came from its membership. The pastors were often looked to as leaders of the religious community. It had a magnificent sanctuary and a fine educational wing.

But in the last few years things had begun to change in the church's neighborhood. It was changing from an upscale, well-to-do section to a low-rent district. Most of the members of the church now drove many miles into the city to worship there, and they were having a hard time attracting new people.

At the leadership meetings you would hear people talk about the great history of this church, but you wouldn't hear anyone talk about adjusting to the new realities of the neighborhood. Their glorious past kept them from moving forward in mission and service.

That same thing can happen with entertainers who keep trying to recapture their past fame, with communities that cannot forget a prosperous past, and with anyone who glorifies the good old days. Focusing on a wonderful past can sometimes keep us from moving on in life.

But sometimes the past that burdens is a hateful deed, or a missed opportunity, not a glorious success. For some the negatives of the past become a problem that haunts us. There are people who cannot forget a wrong committed by someone else. Refusing to forgive, these persons stew in their own poisonous thoughts. There are people who cannot forget a hateful deed they themselves did to another. They flog themselves with the bitter memories of the injuries they caused to others. And there are those who are haunted by the choices they failed to make, or the roads they have taken that have led to dead ends.

Be it glorious or shameful, our past can be a terrible burden that makes it difficult to move on in life. This is something the Jews in the days of Haggai discovered firsthand.

How do we let go of our burdensome past and move on? The Lord gave a threefold answer to that question through Haggai. God told the people this: "Have courage, work, and trust that I am with you."

49

"Have courage" is the first thing Haggai told the people. He was suggesting they begin by working on their attitude. Anyone who has any life experience will readily agree that attitude makes all the difference in the world. If you get up in the morning and expect the worst, you'll probably get a fair share of unpleasant things. But if you face the day with optimism and hope, then you'll probably find all kinds of good things.

In his book *The Informed Heart,* Bruno Bettelheim pointed out that those who went through the concentration camps of World War II discovered that "they still retained the last, if not the greatest, of all the human freedoms: to choose their own attitude in any given circumstance."[1]

The Jews in the days of Haggai had lived through some difficult times. They had spent seventy years in captivity. They came home to find their native country a wasteland. They had enemies who didn't want to see them rebuild the city or the Temple. And they had these memories of a glorious past. If anyone had a right to feel sorry for themselves, it was this group of people.

But the Word of the Lord to them was that they should change their attitude. Be strong. Have courage. Buck up. The prophet knew that if they were going to accomplish anything, they would have to have the proper attitude.

Attitude, as many people have discovered, is a choice we make. It's not something determined by the weather, our health, or the day of the week. Attitude is something we control.

The optimist looks at the glass and sees it as half full; the pessimist sees it as half empty. It's a choice.

The way to work on our attitude is to fill our lives with positive statements and expectations. Expect to perform well, and you will. Expect people to treat you well, and mostly they will. Expect to enjoy life, and you will.

This was so important that the prophet separately urged Zerubbabel, Joshua, and the people all to have courage, to be strong. The prophet knew that starting out with the right attitude is the most important factor in any endeavor.

Edgar Guest wrote a poem that speaks to this issue.

Somebody said that it couldn't be done —
But he with a chuckle replied
That maybe it couldn't but he would be one
Who wouldn't say so till he'd tried.
So he buckled right in, with a bit of a grin
On his face — if he worried he hid it;
He started to sing, as he tackled the thing
That couldn't be done — and he did it!
Somebody scoffed, "Oh, you'll never do that —
At least no one ever has done it."
But he took off his coat and he took off his hat,
And the first thing we knew, he'd begun it.
With a lift of his chin, and a bit of a grin
Without any doubting or "quit it,"
He started to sing, as he tackled the thing
That couldn't be done, and he did it![2]

Our attitude is perhaps the most important factor in any endeavor. It is a choice we make, a choice that no one can take from us. The beginning of laying aside any burden from the past is to have courage, to expect the good.

At the same time we work on our attitude, it's important that we do something for others. God told the people to be strong, but also to work (on the temple). Get your act in gear. Get it done. Don't be so focused on your own needs, problems, and feelings.

Doing something for someone else has a way of changing our melancholy moods. There have been times in my life when I have found that a blue mood has been dispersed by visiting a shut-in or helping someone in some way. Just knowing that I have been helpful to someone else lifts my spirits. It helps me see that the world is a richer, better place because of my presence here. That recognition has to lift anyone's spirit.

We live in a selfish time and culture. Someone is always telling us to do something for ourselves. Take that vacation to the Caribbean. Buy that luxury car. Eat dinner at your favorite restaurant. Do something for yourself.

Often these things don't make us feel better, however. In the long run they may even increase our sadness. People who indulge

51

themselves in this way are not happy. Rather, it is those people who are involved in volunteer service who are the happiest in our society. Giving yourself to others is the way to find the deepest pleasure. To give life meaning, we must have a purpose larger than our own self-interest.

A long time ago, a native Christian was walking with a friend through a howling blizzard in the mountains of north India. They came upon a man lying in the snow, freezing. The friend feared that if he helped the stranger, he would freeze to death, so he left him there. The native Christian, however, picked up the stranger and carried him to the next village.

He made it to the village with the stranger, and discovered that the effort of carrying the man had kept him warm. It had saved his life. Later he discovered that his friend, who had refused to help the stranger, was found frozen to death.

Did not Jesus say something about losing one's life and finding it? Giving one's life and gaining it?

If you want to let go of a burdensome past, get up and do something for someone else. If you can do just one thing well, you're needed somewhere by someone.

Begin by working on your attitude. Do something for someone else. And finally, trust that God will be with you.

The Jews in the time of Haggai must have thought that God had deserted them. God had allowed their temple to be destroyed. God had allowed them to be taken away to Babylon as prisoners of war. God had allowed other people to come and live in the land that had been promised to the descendants of Abraham. There must have been many who believed, even after being allowed to return, that God had forgotten or abandoned them. If that were true, then all their work was in vain.

So the Lord had Haggai give them an important message, an important promise: "Take courage, for I am with you ... My Spirit abides among you."

What the Jewish people had to learn was that disappointment and heartache in life do not mean that God has abandoned us. Misfortune does not mean God does not love us. Pain and suffering do not mean that God has forgotten us.

Time after time God did things for God's people to remind them of God's presence: when God led them out of their Egyptian slavery during the time of Moses; when God gave them the law at Mount Sinai; when God gave them victory over their enemies. And there were tangible things to remind them of God's presence: the pillars of fire and smoke, the Tent of Meeting, the Ark of the Covenant, and the Temple.

But these things were signs and symbols of God's presence. They were never the essence of God's presence. The pillars of fire and smoke ceased after the people ended their travels through the wilderness, but that didn't mean God's presence left them. The Tent of Meeting was replaced by various sanctuaries in the land of Canaan, but that didn't mean God had forgotten them. The Ark of the Covenant and the Temple were destroyed by the Babylonians, but that did not mean that God was absent from their lives.

The exile to Babylon should have taught them that God is with God's people everywhere and always. There is no place we can go that puts us beyond the reach of God's loving arms. There is nothing we can do or experience that drives God out of our lives. In the Christian tradition we have a special reminder of this truth. We believe that God was present in a special way in Jesus Christ. The Incarnation is a story of how God came to be with us.

We further believe that Jesus ascended into heaven so that his Spirit could be with us eternally. Our Lord is not physically present as he was when he walked this earth, but he is spiritually present. As Jesus promised, he is with us always, to the close of the age. And the bread we break and the cup we drink around the Lord's Table are special signs among us that our Lord is here.

What the Jewish people in the days of Haggai really needed was a strong dose of hope. That's what they got in the promise that God was with them.

When we live and work under the assumption that God is with us, that changes everything. It gives us the hope we need to risk difficult challenges. It gives us the courage to go to unknown places. And it gives us the faith to trust that life's darkness will be overcome by the light.

There are times when we may find ourselves as downhearted as the people in the days of Haggai. Sometimes our depression is caused by a burdensome past. But we don't have to remain downhearted. We don't have to let our past mistakes or past glories become a burden. If we work on our attitude by cultivating positive expectations, if we roll up our sleeves and do something for others, and if we trust in God's promise to be with us, then our past will not burden us, and our sadness will not disable us.

With God in our lives, how can we expect anything but the best? With God in our lives, how can we do less than our best? With God in our lives, how can we give less than our best?

---

1. Bruno Bettelheim, *The Informed Heart* (Glencoe, Illinois: The Free Press, 1960), p. 158.

2. Edgar A. Guest, "It Couldn't Be Done," in *The Path to Home* (Chicago: The Reilly & Lee Co., 1919), p. 37.

New And Improved

Proper 28   *Isaiah 65:17-25*
Pentecost 26
Ordinary Time 33

In an effort to capture a bigger share of the consumer market, companies are always trying to improve their products, or at least give us the impression they have improved something. "New and improved" has been a major advertising claim for years.

In recent years "new and improved" has meant such things as taking the color out of detergents, cleaning products, and soda pop, and making these things appear clear in the package. The clear look was supposed to make people think that the product was pure and somehow less filled with artificial additives. A close look at the content of these things, however, revealed that only the color had changed. There was very little new, and not much improvement, if any.

More recently, some of the cleaning products and laundry detergents have gone to smaller packages with a more concentrated product. What's "new and improved" here is that they are using less packaging material and thus are friendlier to the environment. That's worthy of praise. Of course, if you happen to use more of the product than necessary because you are used to the old formula and thus have to buy more of their product, they aren't going to complain.

What is advertised as "new and improved" in our consumer society is often just another attempt to get us to buy a product. "New and improved" is often an empty promise.

In the political scene, events have taken place in the past decade that made it seem that we were headed toward a "new and improved" world. When the communist governments in eastern Europe began to crumble and fall, symbolized by the dismantling of the Berlin Wall, there was great euphoria in the western democracies. The greatest opponent of western democratic capitalism crumbled almost overnight. It was a great victory for democracy.

This sudden change in the world political scene led some to imagine that we were entering a new golden era of peace and prosperity. The Cold War was over! Those who had been our enemies for fifty years now wanted to become our friends! As far as we could tell, the world looked like a "new and improved" place. No more confrontation between the Soviet Union and the United States. No more worries about the domino theory of nations falling under the spell of communism. No more worrying about sending our sons and daughters off to war in some unknown place to stop communism.

It certainly did look like a "new and improved" world — for a while. And then the reality of this new world hit us like a ton of bricks. Without the firm hand of the Soviet Union to keep things under control, ethnic warfare broke out in Bosnia, Russian Georgia, and other places formerly governed by the Kremlin.

Instead of worrying about the nuclear threat of the Soviet Union, we now have to worry about several other former Soviet states that have access to nuclear weapons. And because they are strapped for cash, we have to worry about them selling this technology and material to third world nations.

We still have problems in the Middle East. There is civil war in several African nations. And we are haunted by the specter of terrorism around the world.

Since the fall of communism in Europe, the world certainly is a different place, but it's hardly "new and improved." A different set of problems has replaced the old ones.

Every generation seems to place its hope in certain changes that occur or that people seek to bring about. If only these changes would take place, people feel the world would be a better place.

Woodrow Wilson worked hard for the League of Nations. Lyndon B. Johnson worked hard to create a New Society. The Republicans have worked hard to institute their Contract With America. But no matter how great these efforts may be, they always seem to disappoint us. When all is said and done in political changes, medical discoveries, or technological advances, the world is rarely "new and improved." We may move on to a new set of problems, new characters on the stage of life, but the same old plot comes back again and again.

That plot is a story of human beings polluting, corrupting, and destroying the world God has given us. The story of the Fall from the book of Genesis tells us that we always mess up, even when we live in Paradise.

Nobody had a better shot at living the fullest, most abundant life possible than the people of Israel. God had given them the land of Canaan. God had given them the law and had shown them how to live in a covenant relationship in the land God had given them. But they messed up, and ended up living in Babylon as captives.

When they returned, they hoped everything would be perfect. They had high hopes for a "new and improved" world. They, themselves, had the best intentions, and wanted to do things the right way.

But because of the way we are as fallible human beings, and the way the world is — tainted by our sinfulness — they discovered their life in Jerusalem was not the "new and improved" life for which they had hoped. It was the same old thing. Husbands abused their wives. Merchants cheated customers in the marketplace. People got married but refused to honor their promise of faithfulness. Disease took its toll, and many children died long before they fulfilled their promise. It was not what they were looking for when they returned to their beloved city of God.

So the Lord sent them a message through the prophet. It was a message about the new creation, a message about how things will be when God makes them "new and improved."

As we struggle with our own understanding of the world and our hopes for a brighter future, the message of Isaiah 65 has much to say to us about the new creation.

The first thing we note about the new creation is that it is something God will bring about. It is not something brought about by hard-working Christian people. It is not something brought about by the United Nations, or the United Federation of Planets, or any other human organization that may come into existence. Note the words: "For I am about to create new heavens and a new earth ..." (Isaiah 65:17a). It is something God will do. So many well-intentioned efforts in this world have ended up in disaster because people thought they were bringing in the kingdom, or moving toward the new creation.

The Crusades were well-intentioned efforts to "save" the Holy Land from "heathens," but they turned out to be senseless wars that took life from many innocent people.

The Inquisition was a well-intentioned effort to preserve the true faith and destroy heresy, but it turned out to be a bloody, heartless movement that tortured thousands of fine Christian people.

Even the missionary movement of the nineteenth century started out as an effort to bring all people to faith in Jesus Christ, but there were occasions when native peoples had their own cultures destroyed or needlessly maligned because of the cultural prejudice of Western missionaries.

We are not going to usher in the kingdom of God by our own efforts. We are not capable of creating the new heaven and earth. When it happens, it will be God's work.

Jesus did not tell us to work to bring in the kingdom. He taught us to pray that the kingdom might come. Our job is to pray "thy kingdom come." Leave the details and the success to God. When the "new and improved" creation comes, it will be God's doing.

The second thing we note about the new creation, as described in Isaiah 65, is that it does not involve the total destruction of this creation, but rather its renewal or transformation. This suggests that there is much in this world that is worth saving. If that were

58

not the case, God would want to start all over again, instead of renewing what is already here.

Whenever we talk about the new creation, God's kingdom, or the second coming of Christ, it is tempting to bad-mouth this world so much that we forget to see the good already at work in the world. We are tempted to see only the crime, war, broken relationships, and social disarray that are so prevalent today.

But the vision in Isaiah 65 builds on what is already here and partially experienced. The vision promises long life. If life did not have some sweetness to it, why would we hope for extended life?

The vision promises that those who build houses will live in them, and those who plant vineyards will enjoy the fruit of their labor. If we did not experience some joy and goodness in our homes, why would we hope to live in those which we build? If we did not enjoy food and drink, why would it matter if we eat from gardens and vineyards that we have planted?

The vision promises that mothers will no longer worry about what the future holds for their children. If we did not cherish our children, why would we care about their destiny in life?

It is because we experience some sweetness in life, some joy and happiness, some fulfillment and contentment, that we can deplore a world where these things are absent, and look forward to a world where these things are present in abundance for everyone. The new creation will not obliterate everything we have known and experienced. It will renew and transform the world as we know it. It will take the best of this creation and build on it. It will be "new and improved" in the truest and best sense.

Finally, to say that we are looking forward to the new creation is a statement of faith. To put our hope in this vision is one of the biggest steps of faith we can take, for all around us there are signs of the corrupted, decaying old creation. There are tears, premature death, broken relationships, and all kinds of heartache. It is tough to imagine a better world in the midst of such suffering.

A pastor had a telephone conversation with a young woman recently. She called and asked him to pray for her dog. She asked if that was an acceptable thing to do.

The pastor began to tell her that she didn't have the money to afford a dog. The dog was in the animal hospital right then and she would have to pay the bill. She was going to move because where she lived wasn't a good place for her pet. He told her she couldn't afford to move.

As they continued to talk, this woman had a rare moment of unusual clarity about her life when she answered his advice about getting rid of her dog.

"Pastor, that dog means everything to me. I've never gotten married and didn't get pregnant, like my sisters, so I don't have kids like they do. That dog is my life. My family doesn't care for me. I don't have any friends. That dog is the only thing in the world that loves me. If something happens to that dog, I'll end my life."

After their conversation, the pastor reported that he prayed for her dog. He prayed all week for that dog.

In a world where there are people like that, people who suffer unbelievable emotional pain, to say that we believe in the new creation is an act of the strongest faith. It is not something we can prove. It is not something we can guarantee. It is something we hope for, something we long for, something we look for because God has promised it.

The world around us is always changing. Sometimes we may think those changes are making the world "new and improved." But usually those changes just bring a new set of problems, as the people of Israel discovered.

The only time this world will be "new and improved" is when God ushers in the new creation promised in Isaiah 65. That new creation does not depend on our efforts. It is the work of God. It will take the best of this world and make it even better, as it renews the goodness already present. But it is something for which we are still waiting. It will come in God's time. In the meantime, we are called to trust that what God has promised, God will do.

What really distinguishes us as the people of God is that we never abandon our hope and faith that one day there will be a new heaven and a new earth.

Remembering
Who We Are

Recently, a college basketball player got hurt in a game. It was her third or fourth concussion in recent play. Officials and medical personnel were alarmed when they discovered that the young woman had a selective amnesia as a result of the injury. She knew her name and her family, but she could not recall ever playing basketball. They took her back home and showed her the high school she played for, and she laughed. She didn't believe them when they insisted she played basketball. She forgot who she was, at least in terms of her sport.

Forgetting who we are is a tragic thing. It is so tragic that we spend a great deal of energy in reminding ourselves who we are. The patriotic celebrations we plan for national holidays are partly an attempt to remind us of our democratic heritage. The family reunions that are so prevalent in our communities are an attempt to keep our ethnic and family identities alive. Even the political elections that take place is this country are an attempt to sort out and reinforce who we are as a people. We always want to remember who we are.

Remembering who we are is what worship is all about for the Christian community. One of the main purposes of worship is to clearly identify, clarify, and recall who we are — people created, redeemed, and sustained by a loving God.

In the book of Deuteronomy instructions were given to the people of Israel in regard to worshiping the Lord in the land of promise. When they came to the place of worship, they were to do two things, according to this passage. Both these actions were geared to helping the Israelites remember who they were.

The two things they were to do as part of their worship were these: give their first fruits to the Lord, and tell the story of their salvation history. Give, and tell the story. This is how we help ourselves remember who we are.

The Israelites were instructed to give their first fruits to the Lord. First fruit giving in an agricultural community means giving to God from the first of one's harvest, not the last. The first grain that was harvested was given to God. They didn't wait until they had harvested every field and saw how much they had and what the quality was like. Before they knew what they would have after the harvest, God got a share.

This is living by faith. This is what it means to be the people of God. Giving from our first fruits teaches us to trust in God for all we need.

People who worry about having enough aren't going to give to God out of first fruits. They will wait and see what is left over after all their needs and wants are satisfied, and then decide if they can give something to God.

That may be good enough for those outside the faith, but for those who have experienced the salvation wrought by God, for those who have been led from bondage to freedom, it simply won't do. The people of God live by faith, and so we give our first fruits, trusting that God will take care of all our needs.

Giving our first fruits reminds us that we are people who have experienced the saving power of God in our lives. It reminds us that we are called to be people who live by faith, not by the assurance of a barn filled to overflowing with grain and corn.

This kind of faith is what enables the trapeze artist to leave one trapeze bar and reach for another being swung his or her way. It is to leave the security of one place in order to take hold of something else.

To give in this way, with our first fruits, is to show God the honor and glory that is his due. It is to demonstrate that we are people of faith.

This kind of giving should be seen to include more than our money or harvest. It includes our time and talents as well. We give to God our best; we give to God first, and then take care of the other demands in our lives.

The other thing called for in worship from this passage is the retelling of the story of salvation. Every time we worship we retell a part of the story. That's how we remember who we are. Someone has said that the Christian Church is always just one generation away from extinction. If we fail to tell the story, we will suffer from amnesia, and forget who we are.

For the people of Israel, the story began with the words, "A wandering Aramean was my ancestor; he went down into Egypt and lived there as an alien ..." (Deuteronomy 26:5b). The affirmation of faith includes the story of the oppression by the Egyptians, and the subsequent release from bondage accomplished through God's outstretched arm. Telling the story reminded the Israelites of who they were.

We have a gospel song by Katharine Hankey that reads like this:

> *Tell me the old, old story*
> *Of unseen things above,*
> *Of Jesus and his glory,*
> *Of Jesus and his love.*
> *Tell me the story simply,*
> *As to a little child,*
> *For I am weak and weary,*
> *And helpless and defiled.*
>
> *Tell me the story slowly,*
> *That I may take it in —*
> *That wonderful redemption,*
> *God's remedy for sin.*
> *Tell me the story often,*
> *For I forget so soon ...*

Tell me the story softly,
  With earnest tones and grave;
  Remember, I'm the sinner
  Whom Jesus came to save....

In the Christian community, no less than in the Hebrew community, we must constantly remind ourselves who we are, for it is easy to forget. When we're driving down the road and someone cuts in front of us and forces us to slam on the brakes, it's easy to forget who we are and come out with some four-letter expletive. When we're at college for the first year and exploring our new-found freedom, it's easy to forget who we are and do things we never would have dreamed of doing at home. When business is tough, and the competition is murderous, it's easy to forget our ethics and do things that aren't right, just to improve our performance.

Some pastors always wear a clerical collar when they go to visit people in the hospital. It identifies them as a pastor and gets them in to the places they need to go with ease and deference. The collar also reminds them of who they are. Some even find that they are always a bit more careful when they wear that collar, for they don't want to bring shame or criticism to the name of Jesus.

Some people find that crosses do the same thing for them, or bumper stickers on their car. These things remind them of who they are.

We are a people saved by grace.

We are a people who live by faith.

We are a people loved by God.

We are a people redeemed by the blood of the lamb, people for whom Jesus died on the cross.

We are a people called to a new way of life.

We are a people who turn the other cheek, people who go the extra mile, people who give without thought for reward.

We are a people who love our enemies and forgive those who hurt us. People who delay our journey so we can help the wounded person who sits on the side of the road.

We are people who hold fast to what is good, and render to no one evil for evil. People who strengthen the fainthearted, who support the weak, help the suffering, and honor all people.

Telling the story in the context of worship reminds us of who we are.

So we are called by this passage to be givers and storytellers. Our giving helps us become the people of faith that we are, by nature. Giving our first fruits requires that we put our trust in God. And the telling of our story, God's story, calls forth our best. These are the ways we remember who we are.

Promises Kept
In Unusual Ways

General Douglas MacArthur was one of the great heroes of World War II. He was greatly admired by many people, and well loved by the people of the Philippines. One reason for the admiration and love was that he kept an important promise. When the Japanese invasion forced MacArthur to retreat from the Philippines, he promised he would return. Standing in the water in March 1942, before he embarked on a voyage to the safety of Australia, the general promised, "I shall return." And he did.

In October 1944, when he landed on the islands, MacArthur spoke the words that meant so much to the Philippine people. "I have returned. By the grace of Almighty God, our forces stand again on Philippine soil." He had kept his word. He had fulfilled his promise.

One of the things that we generally admire in people is honesty and integrity. When people give us their word, we like to be able to depend on it. When a teenager tells his parents he will be home by 11:00 p.m., they want to be able to trust that he'll come in the door by that set time. When a fellow worker says she'll get something done, her co-workers want to know they can count on her following through and keeping her word. When a preacher says he'll have you out by noon, we like to be able to depend on it.

It is a wonderful thing to be able to take someone's word and count on it. And it is precisely the lack of integrity in current politics that makes the political scene so distasteful to many of us. There doesn't seem to be a politician alive who can keep his or her word. They will tell us anything to get elected. Once they are in office, they seem to do whatever they please and forget the promises they made during the election campaign.

We like to be able to take others at their word. A promise kept goes a long way to enhancing personal relationships of all kinds. The husband and wife who are faithful to each other can endure all kinds of outside stress because even if they can't count on others, they can count on each other. The friends who keep their promises to each other have relationships that last a lifetime. And the companies that keep their promises to their workers have loyal employees that give their best.

We have a God who is faithful, a God who always keeps God's word, a God who never betrays our trust. When God makes a promise, that promise is always kept. That is a fundamental idea of the Christian faith. God is faithful. We can count on God being true.

In fact, the whole history of God's people in the Bible is a history of God being faithful to God's word. God promised Abraham and Sarah that they would be the parents of a mighty nation and that all the world would be blessed through them. Those promises were kept. God promised that their descendants would possess the land of Canaan. That promise was kept.

Later on, when God's people were slaves in Egypt, God appeared to Moses and called him to be God's special servant and bring the people out of their bondage. Moses made several excuses, but God promised to be with Moses and to give him the help he would need. That promise was kept, and the people were liberated from their Egyptian servitude.

Many years later, God promised to make David king over the people of Israel, and to have David's descendants rule over God's people in the land of Judah. As long as there was a kingdom in Judah up till 586 B.C., David's descendants sat on the throne.

Time after time, in big ways and in little ways, the Bible has shown us that God can be trusted. When God promises to do something, God always follows through. Our God is faithful.

In the passage from Jeremiah 23:1-6, God promises through the prophet to do two things: to gather the remnant of God's people (who had been dispersed after the Babylonian victory), and to raise up a new shepherd, a king who will execute justice.

This passage was obviously addressed to the Jews living in exile. In their situation, they needed some kind of hope. The very foundation of their lives had been destroyed with the unimaginable Babylonian victory and conquest of Jerusalem.

Psalm 137 captures the mood of the Jewish people well.

By the rivers of Babylon —
  there we sat down and there we wept
  when we remembered Zion.
On the willows there we hung up our harps.
For there our captors asked us for songs,
  and our tormentors asked for mirth, saying,
  "Sing us one of the songs of Zion!"
How could we sing the Lord's song in a foreign land?

Psalm 137: 1- 4

At this point in time, Jeremiah's message changed from one of condemnation and judgment to one of hope. The people who wept in Babylon could count on God bringing them back to their homeland, and giving them a new king who would fill the land with justice and righteousness.

This new king, according to Jeremiah, will reign as king. This is a curious thing to say about a king, until we take into account the political situation. The king at this time was Zedekiah, who was a true descendant of David, but was really just a puppet of the Babylonian king. He had no real power of his own. The righteous Branch from David, however, will have the power of a real king, and will use that power to establish and maintain justice.

The people living at this time expected God to keep this promise. They knew that God is faithful. But what they did not know at the time was that God was going to fulfill this promise in an unusual way. God brought the Jews back to Jerusalem after an exile that lasted about 70 years, but the king mentioned here was not raised up at that time.

The fulfillment of this promise came about when God sent the Son to the earth, when Jesus was born. The surprise is that God's king did not rule with political or military power. The Messianic King turned out to be the Crucified Messiah, much to the surprise of everyone.

The Jews, at the time of Jesus, were expecting a Messiah who would come and drive out the Roman conquerors and establish a powerful kingdom that would make all the nations cower with fear. They expected that all the world's people would come and worship their King in Jerusalem. They expected that his kingdom would have no end.

What they got, instead, was a man who was crucified on the cross, a man put to death by his own people because he dared to challenge the status quo, a man who died a humiliating death to save us from our sins. It was not at all what they expected. But it was what we all needed.

God keeps God's word, but not always in ways we would expect. Sometimes God surprises us in the ways in which God's promises are kept. When God led the people of Israel into the promised land, God led them the long way around. Apparently, they had a lot to learn before they entered the land of promise.

God will not be put in a box; God will not be bound by our expectations. God is free to keep promises any way God wants to, even if they are strange and unexpected ways.

What was true in the time of Jeremiah is still true today. God can be trusted to keep God's word, but not always in the way we expect.

For example, God has promised to be with us, and we often interpret that promise to mean that God will not let any harm come to us. That's a wonderful promise to cling to, but there's not a person here who has not known some heartache, disappointment, or tragedy in life. God's presence with us does not always shield us from those things, as we sometimes expect, but often it means that God will walk with us through our heartache and pain.

70

A little girl was in the hospital with a serious illness. They were doing everything they could medically, but they were losing the battle. Her parents stayed with her constantly. When she slipped into a coma, they continued to stay with her, holding her hand, talking to her, making sure someone was in the room 24 hours a day.

After four days in a coma, the girl miraculously woke up and started to improve. The doctors could not explain her recovery. When her parents talked to her about the experience, the little girl assured them that she had not been afraid. She told them, "I knew you were with me, and that gave me courage. I wasn't afraid as long as you were here."

Psalm 23 says, "Even though I walk through the darkest valley, I fear no evil; for you are with me...."

God is not going to shield us from all the heartache and pain of life. There will be times when we have to embrace our fair share of discomfort and suffering. But God is with us in our pain, in our heartache, in our disappointment. Is that not what it means to have a Crucified Messiah? The presence of God in our lives gives us courage and hope, even if it doesn't take away the pain.

God does not always keep God's word in ways we would expect. But God is always faithful. And that faithfulness is what enables us to be people filled with hope.

A husband and wife made it a point every year to take their children on a nice family vacation. It had become a tradition with them, and it was one thing that made their family so strong.

One year the husband was very busy with his work. It didn't look like he would be able to get away for a vacation that year. But they made plans anyway, hoping things would work out.

When it came time for the vacation, the husband just could not get away. But he helped them load the car, and sent them on their way. He promised to join them when he could.

He went back to his job and worked all day and all night to finish what had to be done. Then he jumped on a plane and flew to the family's vacation destination. He took a cab and had the driver let him off on the road he knew his family would be taking. There he stood for several hours, waiting for their car to come by. When he saw it, he held out his thumb and hitched a ride with his wife and children.

He had kept his word. He had kept it in an unusual, unexpected and memorable way, to be sure. But he kept his promise.

We like to have people like that in our lives: people who keep their word no matter what. But what's more important is that we have a God in our lives who keeps God's word. The Bible is nothing less than the story of God's faithfulness. God did raise up a righteous Branch from the house of David, as was promised. God did establish God's throne forever. God has, indeed, crowned this king with honor and glory. But God did this in God's own way. The Messianic King turned out to be the Crucified Messiah. Not what God's people expected, but exactly what we needed.

This teaches us to expect God not only to keep God's word, but to do so in unexpected and wonderful ways. We tend to put God in a box, and define the ways in which God will be faithful. But God is the one who will teach us the true meaning of all God's promises.

Lectionary Preaching
After Pentecost

The following index will aid the user of this book in matching the correct Sunday with the appropriate text during Pentecost. All texts in this book are from the series for Lesson One, Revised Common Lectionary. (Note that the ELCA division of Lutheranism is now following the Revised Common Lectionary.) The Lutheran and Roman Catholic designations indicate days comparable to Sundays on which Revised Common Lectionary Propers are used.

(Fixed dates do not pertain to Lutheran Lectionary)

Fixed Date Lectionaries *Revised Common (including ELCA)* *and Roman Catholic*	Lutheran Lectionary *Lutheran*
The Day of Pentecost	The Day of Pentecost
The Holy Trinity	The Holy Trinity
May 29-June 4 — Proper 4, Ordinary Time 9	Pentecost 2
June 5-11 — Proper 5, Ordinary Time 10	Pentecost 3
June 12-18 — Proper 6, Ordinary Time 11	Pentecost 4
June 19-25 — Proper 7, Ordinary Time 12	Pentecost 5
June 26-July 2 — Proper 8, Ordinary Time 13	Pentecost 6
July 3-9 — Proper 9, Ordinary Time 14	Pentecost 7
July 10-16 — Proper 10, Ordinary Time 15	Pentecost 8
July 17-23 — Proper 11, Ordinary Time 16	Pentecost 9
July 24-30 — Proper 12, Ordinary Time 17	Pentecost 10
July 31-Aug. 6 — Proper 13, Ordinary Time 18	Pentecost 11
Aug. 7-13 — Proper 14, Ordinary Time 19	Pentecost 12
Aug. 14-20 — Proper 15, Ordinary Time 20	Pentecost 13
Aug. 21-27 — Proper 16, Ordinary Time 21	Pentecost 14
Aug. 28-Sept. 3 — Proper 17, Ordinary Time 22	Pentecost 15
Sept. 4-10 — Proper 18, Ordinary Time 23	Pentecost 16
Sept. 11-17 — Proper 19, Ordinary Time 24	Pentecost 17

Sept. 18-24 — Proper 20, Ordinary Time 25	Pentecost 18
Sept. 25-Oct. 1 — Proper 21, Ordinary Time 26	Pentecost 19
Oct. 2-8 — Proper 22, Ordinary Time 27	Pentecost 20
Oct. 9-15 — Proper 23, Ordinary Time 28	Pentecost 21
Oct. 16-22 — Proper 24, Ordinary Time 29	Pentecost 22
Oct. 23-29 — Proper 25, Ordinary Time 30	Pentecost 23
Oct. 30-Nov. 5 — Proper 26, Ordinary Time 31	Pentecost 24
Nov. 6-12 — Proper 27, Ordinary Time 32	Pentecost 25
Nov. 13-19 — Proper 28, Ordinary Time 33	Pentecost 26
	Pentecost 27
Nov. 20-26 — Christ the King	Christ the King

Reformation Day (or last Sunday in October) is October 31 (Revised Common, Lutheran)

All Saints' Day (or first Sunday in November) is November 1 (Revised Common, Lutheran, Roman Catholic)

Books In This Cycle C Series

Gospel Set
Sermons For Advent/Christmas/Epiphany
Deep Joy For A Shallow World
Richard A. Wing

Sermons For Lent/Easter
Taking The Risk Out Of Dying
Lee Griess

Sermons For Pentecost I
The Chain Of Command
Alexander H. Wales

Sermons For Pentecost II
All Stirred Up
Richard W. Patt

Sermons For Pentecost III
Good News Among The Rubble
J. Will Ormond

First Lesson Set
Sermons For Advent/Christmas/Epiphany
Where Is God In All This?
Tony Everett

Sermons For Lent/Easter
Returning To God
Douglas J. Deuel

Sermons For Pentecost I
How Long Will You Limp?
Carlyle Fielding Stewart, III

Sermons For Pentecost II
Lord, Send The Wind
James McLemore

Sermons For Pentecost III
Buying Swamp Land For God
Robert P. Hines, Jr.

www.ingramcontent.com/pod-product-compliance
Lightning Source LLC
Chambersburg PA
CBHW060144050426
42448CB00010B/2295